THE KUGB G
BETTER KA

Published in the same series by Pan Books

The PGA European Tour Guide to Better Golf
The LTA Guide to Better Tennis
The British Ski Federation Guide to Better Skiing
The Amateur Athletic Association Guide to Better Athletics
The Amateur Swimming Association Guide to Better Swimming
The SRA/WSRA Guide to Better Squash
The Neil Adams Guide to Better Judo

THE KUGB
GUIDE TO BETTER
KARATE

BOB POYNTON
CAESAR ANDREWS
AND GARY DAY-ELLISON

Photographs by Roy Victor

Pan Books
London, Sydney and Auckland

Contents

Sensei Enoeda	*Foreword*	9
Andy Sherry	*Introduction*	11
I. S. Maclaren	*The history of shotokan karate*	12
	KUGB dojo rules and etiquette	14
	Karate grading	16
	KUGB grading rules	17
Brad Williamson	*Karate fitness and medical advice*	18
	Editors' note	19

FUNDAMENTALS

Bob Poynton	*Introduction*	21
Bob Poynton	*Dachi (stances)*	23
	Zenkutsu dachi	
	Kokutsu dachi	
	Kiba dachi	

Bob Rhodes *Uke (blocks)* 29

    Gedan barai
    Age uke
    Soto ude uke
    Uche ude uke
    Shuto uke

Andy Sherry *Tsuki (punches)* 41

    Choku zuki
    Oi zuki
    Kizami zuki
    Gyaku zuki

Terry O'Neill *Keri waza (kicks)* 49

    Mae geri
    Yoko geri kekomi
    Yoko geri keage
    Mawashi geri
    Ushiro geri

Bob Poynton *Uchi waza (strikes)* 61

    Shuto uchi
    Haito uchi
    Uraken uchi
    Nukite
    Tettsui uchi
    Yoko empi uchi
    Age empi uchi
    Mawashi empi uchi
    Otoshi empi uchi

Billy Higgins *Ashi barai (sweeps)* 73

    Ashi barai, oi zuki
    Ashi barai, gyaku zuki

KATA (PREARRANGED FORMS)

Frank Brennan　　　*Introduction*　　　77

　　　Kihon kata
　　　Heian shodan
　　　Heian nidan
　　　Heian sandan
　　　Heian yondan
　　　Heian godan
　　　Tekki shodan
　　　Bassai dai

KUMITE (SPARRING)

Bob Poynton　　　*Introduction*　　　141

　　　Gohon kumite
　　　Kihon ippon kumite
　　　Jiyu ippon kumite

Karen Findley　　　*Jiyu kumite*　　　155

　　　Glossary of Japanese terms　　　158

Dedication

This book is dedicated to Sensei
Keinosuke Enoeda whose technique,
spirit and teaching skills are an
inspiration to all, and whose work for
karate over the years has made all things
possible: it is a tremendous achievement
we can only gratefully acknowledge.

Foreword

Sensei Enoeda, 8th dan, is the representative in the United Kingdom of the Japan Karate Association (JKA), and chief instructor to the Karate Union of Great Britain and Europe.

There is a saying: 'Karate starts with courtesy and finishes with courtesy.' This maxim is the most important thing in karate-do (the way of karate). Unfortunately, courtesy is often distorted. It should be shown naturally, from the first. It is not true courtesy if it is a mere observance of forms, based on class divisions. Moreover, it is unreasonable to insist on courtesy from others. It originates from yourself, and you cannot be a true karateka until you are fully aware of the meaning of these words in your everyday life.

Karate is a martial art, and like all art it requires the same deep study and constant striving for perfection. Karate has always been purely a form of self-defence and a means to improve one's fitness and mental attitude. Fighting in karate is *always* controlled. Too many people assume that the main point is to learn fighting skills. This is the wrong attitude. To those people I say, if you are starting karate for this, then it is a limited attitude, and you should not be in this sport.

Keinosuke Enoeda (left)

It is fundamental that karate should be practised in the true spirit of the martial arts. Sports karate is a recent development in this ancient art, and it should not form a predominant part of the true karateka's outlook. It can have its detractions. With sports karate, formerly the emphasis was on keeping a strong controlled technique, but now it is more on match-winning techniques, lessening the importance attached to the need for good solid blocking. This is a pity. I believe that we must still employ powerful techniques because if we do not and think only in terms of competition, the result will be that the real discipline of karate will be destroyed and it will become just another sport. Therefore, for someone committed to competition within the larger context of practising karate, it is vital to work hard at basics in order to develop later a strong and correct competition fighting technique. There must be hard training and commitment.

Teachers must educate their students correctly by putting equal emphasis on all aspects of karate. I am fortunate in having received instruction from both the father and founder of modern shotokan, Sensei Funakoshi, and the late great Sensei Nakayama. They emphasized to me how mental training and good self-discipline are strictly necessary in a dojo, and one must always show proper conduct by setting a good example and observing fully the regulations of the dojo code. The benefits which are achieved through a good attitude to the real meaning of all karate are of the greatest importance, and help also to improve your attitudes not solely inside the dojo but also in all other aspects of your life. I consider the saying *'Karate ni sente nashi'* (In karate you never take the initiative) very illustrative of the correct approach which good karate should induce. Behind this saying lies the spirit of karate-do, which is essentially good will and respect towards all humanity. With this in mind I hope, regardless of age or ability, you will derive considerable satisfaction from the many new challenges you will encounter.

Keinosuke Enoeda wins the all Japan kumite championships, 1963

Introduction

Andy Sherry, 6th dan, is the chairman and a founder member of the KUGB, and chief British instructor. He is a former European and British champion, and current coach and manager to the KUGB British team.

The Karate Union of Great Britain (KUGB) is the largest single karate organization in the United Kingdom, practising the shotokan system of karate. It has grown since its inception in 1966 and now has more than 20,000 members practising in over 440 clubs.

The KUGB's primary aim is the development of high technical standards and to this end has acquired the services of Master Keinosuke Enoeda 8th dan as its chief instructor together with numerous other high grade instructors including those featured in this book. The KUGB always stresses that karate is not only a physical art, and teaches the importance of the development of the character through hard and dedicated training. Indeed, the dojo code of the KUGB is character, sincerity, effort, etiquette and self-control.

This publication lays out the basic structure of shotokan karate and the KUGB's senior instructors demonstrate the techniques in an easy-to-understand way. It must be stressed, however, that karate can only be developed to a high level by training under a competent instructor and hopefully this book will be the reader's inspiration to joining a KUGB karate club and pursuing their studies further.

Keinosuke Enoeda teaching at National Sports Centre, Norwood

I. S. MACLAREN

The History of Shotokan Karate

I. S. Maclaren, 3rd dan, is an expert on the history of karate and the martial arts, and the author of several books.

Shotokan karate is one of the most popular of modern styles. It is the most powerful and dynamic of the Japanese systems, and is generally considered to be the most comprehensive, both in the range of its techniques and the number and diversity of its kata. But to understand the basis of shotokan, and to see the rich pedigree of karate, we need to look to its origins.

The first concrete evidence of unarmed fighting methods appears on the tomb of Pharoah Menes, the warrior king who first unified Egypt and who died around 3,000 BC. Pictures show an unarmed combat technique which karateka would recognize as jodan uke in shiko dachi (a block to the face area, warrior in square stance). The Chinese emperor Shi-Huang-Di (221–206 BC) was buried with an army of some 7,000 life-size figures of horses and soliders to guard him in the afterlife, and of particular interest are the figures of the officers, all unarmed and in postures showing they used a fighting method remarkably similar to karate. Throughout this period and after, the Chinese countryside was rife with bandits, and merchants hired bodyguards to protect their caravans. This eventually led to the development of the professional warrior, and it was under conditions such as these that the martial arts evolved in the East.

The Ryukyu Islands, known to us as Okinawa, played a prominent role in karate's history. Formerly an independent kingdom, they became a Chinese vassal state in 1372, and when all weapons were banned in 1429, there was a tremendous secret development of empty-hand fighting. In 1609 the islands were conquered by Japan and all weapons and martial arts were again banned; this again ensured the art's development to a formidable degree of efficiency. Most karate history has come down to us by word of mouth, and there are many tales of the great Okinawan karateka. The term karate first appeared in 1772, when an Okinawan called Sakugawa started to teach what he called *karate-no-sakagawa*.

Shotokan is a modern name given to the style of karate that developed from the Okinawan systems, and which was introduced to Japan in 1922 by Gichin Funakoshi, the 'father of modern karate'. He was born in 1868, and studied karate from his childhood. His love of the art led the Okinawan to teach. Funakoshi first arrived in Japan in 1922, invited by the Japanese Ministry of Education to attend an athletic exhibition. His demonstration of karate was a great success, and while he remained unknown for a few more years, he was befriended by the founder of judo, Jigero

Kano. Kano's help made a great impression on him, and he never forgot his kindness. The respect and courtesy he was shown probably influenced his own teaching and philosophy.

Between 1926 and 1930, Funakoshi developed karate further and consolidated its position in Japan. The universities were the main sites of karate study, and they were influenced by research on physiology and calisthenics. During this period Funakoshi and his son Yoshitaka added kumite (fighting) methods, the Japanese kyu/dan ranking system, and some of the traditional concepts of budo (martial way) to the system. Under Yoshitaka, the development of shotokan karate really accelerated. The stances were studied and strengthened by being made lower so as to apply dynamic controlled stress to the leg muscles, and the effect of hip rotation on punches and kicks was also examined. This resulted in an increase in the power of punching and kicking techniques. This knowledge was incorporated into the kihon (basics) of shotokan karate. After 1936, the kata (sequences of movements) were revised to conform to the dynamic new style.

The word 'shotokan' was chosen by Funakoshi's students to name his first personal dojo, and it derives from his pen name, 'shoto', meaning 'pine waves', and 'kan', meaning hall. It soon became the name for Funakoshi's style of karate.

Yoshitaka Funakoshi died in early 1945, his death probably precipitated by the news that his father's dojo had been destroyed in a bombing raid. After the war, Funakoshi returned to teaching in Tokyo, and in 1952, at the age of eighty four, he undertook a three-month tour of American air bases, thus ensuring the spread of shotokan karate to America. He died in 1957. His memorial bears the words *'Karate ni sente nashi'* – 'There is no first attack in karate'.

KUGB Dojo Rules and Etiquette

1 Bow on entering and leaving the dojo.

2 Address any instructor as 'Sensei' whilst in the dojo.

3 'Oss' is a sign of respect and is used generally in karate especially in the following situations –

(*i*) Upon receiving any advice or command from the instructor, the student must reply by answering 'Oss'.

(*ii*) When bowing at the start and finish of the class.

(*iii*) When bowing to your partner during kumite.

(*iv*) In any other appropriate situation, for instance during gradings or competitions.

4 Train at least twice a week.

5 No one is to leave the class without first obtaining permission from the instructor before the start of the class.

6 Any member arriving late must take up a kneeling position at the front of the dojo and await permission from the instructor before joining the class.

On receiving permission, bow and then join the class.

7 Finger and toe nails must be kept clean and short.

8 Gis must be kept clean and in good condition.

9 Jewellery (rings, bracelets, neck chains etc.) must not be worn during training. If you can't get a ring off then tape must be wrapped around it.

10 Apply for a licence from the Karate Union of Great Britain **immediately** upon being accepted into the dojo.

11 Members must not smoke, swear, chew, spit or commit any other act likely to offend the etiquette of the dojo.

12 Members must not use their skills in any offensive way outside the dojo.

The dojo code (opposite) was written with Japanese characters by Sensei Enoeda with the English translation below.

Sensei Enoeda wishes all karateka to endeavour to apply this code throughout their karate training and life.

訓

一、人格完成に努むること

一、誠の道を守ること

一、努力の精神を養うこと

一、礼儀を重んずること

一、血気の勇を戒むること

榎枝慶之輔

| Refrain from impetuous and violent behaviour | Respect propriety | Cultivate the spirit of perseverance | Be faithful and sincere | Exert oneself in the perfection of character | Dojo Code |

15

Karate Grading

GRADE	BELT	KATAS (to be performed in order to progress to the next grade)
Novice	White	Kihon kata
9th kyu	Orange	Heian shodan
8th kyu	Red	Heian nidan
7th kyu	Yellow	Heian sandan
6th kyu	Green	Heian yondan
5th kyu	Purple	Heian godan
4th kyu	Purple and white stripe	Tekki shodan
3rd kyu	Brown	Bassai dai

2nd kyu	Brown and white stripe	Bassai dai
1st kyu	Brown and white stripe	Bassai, jihon, hangetsu, kanku dai, empi
1st dan	Black	Bassai sho, kanku sho, niju shiho, tekki nidan

N.B. Sometimes a 'temporary' kyu grade is awarded. This is a pass and entitles the holder to all the facilities applying to that particular grade. However it indicates a 'borderline' pass and the grade must be confirmed at the next examination before progressing to the next level.

To illustrate this a student awarded a temporary 7th kyu will wear a yellow belt and at the next grading may progress to 7th kyu, temporary 6th or full 6th, depending on standard.

KUGB Grading Rules

1   A student must train for a minimum of two months with training at least twice per week in order to take the first grading.

2   From 9th kyu to 1st kyu a minimum period of three months must be allowed with training at least twice per week, between each kyu Grade.

3   A temporary 1st kyu must wait a period of three months before taking full 1st kyu grading then a further six months must be allowed before taking 1st dan grading.

4   A minimum period of six months must be allowed between 1st kyu and 1st dan. (Members must be a full 1st kyu before taking 1st dan grading.)

5   A minimum period of two years must be allowed between shodan to nidan gradings. A minimum period of three years between nidan to sandan gradings.

6   Members failing a dan grading must wait a further period of time as indicated by the grading examiner, before re-grading.

7   Grades taken by members found to be breaking the rules of grading shall not be recognized by the KUGB.

8   Any karateka from other Associations or styles, who join the KUGB, may wear the belt of the grade they have attained in their previous association, but after six months regular training they must take a grading with an approved KUGB examiner, when they will be awarded the appropriate KUGB Grade – (THIS APPLIES **TO ALL GRADES**, INCLUDING BLACK BELTS).

9   All karateka must bring their current licence and record book when taking a grading, as the examiner will refuse to grade any member not able to produce these documents.

BRAD WILLIAMSON

Karate Fitness and Medical Advice

Brad Willliamson FRCS, is the KUGB official team doctor, approved by the European Shotokan Karate Association.

Karate is mentally and physically a highly demanding sport and art. To perform karate properly, it is essential to cultivate a healthy lifestyle. In this respect it does not differ from other disciplines or sports in requiring regular sleep and a balanced diet.

Once started on the karate path a karateka will soon find his fitness increasing. An important requirement is the development and maintenance of maximum mobility and flexibility. This allows the far reach and speed associated with karate techniques (e.g. long punches, high kicks). The first part of each lesson is always devoted to calisthenics and stretching excixes. It is perhaps the most important part of the lesson – if you neglect it, you do so at your peril.

Calisthenics will strengthen and improve the efficiency of the heart and lungs, and thus increase the blood flow to the muscles which you will be using so much later in the class. Stretching exercises gradually develop the suppleness and range of motion of the joints, and help prevent sprains and strains. It is now known that static stretching (i.e. holding a position at maximum stretch) is much more beneficial than ballistic stretching (trying to swing sharply to maximum stretch), as with the latter the body's natural safety mechanisms stop the maximum stretch being reached. Stretching has to be gradual, otherwise muscles will go into spasm. For this reason, it is important that the exercises are performed in warm conditions and on an even surface. Dojos preferably should have a sprung wooden floor which allows good grip and balance, and which also minimizes injuries during stepping or falling.

Once past the warm up, there are two sorts of injury. Firstly there are the knocks and bruises characteristic of any contact sport (although in our experience they are much less common in karate than in rugby, for example). These can be avoided by good control and common sense, in both yourself and your instructor. The second type is the 'overuse' injury, and this is common to all sports. As you may guess, it's caused by repetitive overuse of a muscle. It is much easier to prevent with careful warm up than to treat once it has happened. The essence of treatment is rest. This is probably best supervised by a physiotherapist with an interest in sports injuries.

In summary karate is a sport (some would say a way of life) which is unsurpassed in its potential for building both physical fitness and mental alertness. Provided that a few simple guidelines are adhered to, then the risk of injury is very small.

Editors' Note

You can not learn karate solely from a book. You will learn by regularly attending a good KUGB club, training hard and listening to the instruction of your teachers. Our book is intended as a guide to complement your training in the dojo and to help you practise and study at home.

A good student will soon realize that the more skill you acquire, the more there will still be for you to learn and develop. KUGB instruction, in conjunction with the traditional grading system, is carefully structured to improve gradually your physical condition and mental attitude the more you practise. Train with dedication and constantly try to improve on the fundamentals, and you will be rewarded with results. The true karateka must and will learn *never to abuse their skills*.

Whether you study for fitness, self-defence or competition you will improve your quality of life if you learn well. Enjoy your karate!

Karate maxim:
I promise to uphold the true spirit of karate-do and never to use the skills that I am taught against any persons, except for the defence of myself, family or friends in the instance of extreme danger or unprovoked attack, or in support of law and order.

19

Fundamentals

Bob Poynton, 5th dan, is a senior instructor, grading examiner, and executive officer of the KUGB. He is a former British champion and a member of the KUGB British team.

Introduction

Your karate training will fall into three main categories, these being kihon, kata and kumite.

Kihon means basics and the term covers all the basic blocks, punches, kicks, strikes, sweeps and stances.

Kata are set sequences of basic movements designed to develop balance, strength and concentration. They range from short basic sequences through to very long complicated sequences. They are used as part of the grading system, with certain kata being allied to certain grades. These are listed on page 16.

Kumite is fighting, and different formalized routines are explained which develop attacks, defences, counter-attacks and timing; these are the basic building blocks for freestyle fighting.

Not all techniques, katas, or types of fighting are shown, but all you need up to black belt is contained in this book.

Here are some important points to bear in mind when practising the fundamental techniques. They are consequently of great importance in your kata and kumite.

1 Always stretch slowly and well all parts of the body prior to training (for at least fifteen minutes).
2 Practise the techniques slowly as you are in control, and speed up gradually as you gain confidence and ability.
3 Always keep your head straight and maintain eye contact with your opponent or imaginary opponents.
4 Maximum power will only be obtained by using all possible body motion in conjunction with your technique by, for example, thrusting, stepping or twisting.
5 Never neglect one area of the body when using another – for example, don't drop your guard when kicking.
6 When using arm techniques, always try to employ *both* arms. For example, use one arm to deliver the technique and the other to balance the technique.

A good way of testing the effectiveness of techniques is to practise on an inanimate object, such as a punchbag. In the early stages, use light contact in such practice until you become more proficient.

BOB POYNTON, 5TH DAN

Dachi (Stances)

Introduction

Stances provide stability whilst executing techniques, and allow you to position yourself to deliver those techniques. The way in which you employ them determines your weight distribution and therefore your ability in attacking or retreating. As with all fundamentals, warm up well and practise *slowly* until you gain expertise.

Shotokan stances are practised deep in order to strengthen and make supple the legs and hips. Throughout a step, the upper body should be held controlled but relaxed. Only on completion should all the body be tight and focused. Low stances may seem uncomfortable, but they produce maximum stability and develop strong legs and hips. Never raise the head as this weakens the stance.

The stances here show clearly the distribution of weight predominantly to the front, back or centre. There are other stances which exhibit subtle variation in weight distribution.

You can practise the following from a variety of starting positions, which you will meet in the dojo when you are training under different instructors. But for convenience, in each stance here the demonstrators start with a feet-together position.

ZENKUTSU DACHI (FRONT STANCE)

1 *Starting position: place both hands lightly on your hips as you bring the right foot to meet and touch the left foot. Bend your knees fully, keeping your back straight and looking directly in front.*

2 *Slide the right foot forward and out until you are at the halfway position, keeping hips, arms and back still. Your weight should still be on your left leg. Keep your balance: you must be stable and your movements smooth throughout.*

3 *Drive the right foot all the way forward into the full stance by thrusting strongly from the back leg. Keep your back foot flat and your feet hip-width apart. Your front knee should be directly above your big toe.*

All stances are demonstrated by Frank Brennan

Side view of position **3**.

Turn from position **3**.

1 *Without twisting your hips, move the back leg all the way across as shown. Weight is still on the right (bent) leg.*

2 *Complete the turn by strongly twisting the hips, using the thrusting action of the right leg.*

KOKUTSU DACHI (BACK STANCE)

1 *Starting position: move right foot into hei soku dachi, placing hands on hips. Bend your knees fully, keeping your back straight and looking directly in front.*

2 *Slide your right foot straight forward to the halfway position, keeping the weight on the left leg and the left knee bent fully.*

*Side view of position **3**.*

3   Pivot the hips and use the force of this movement to slide the right foot all the way forward, retaining approximately 70% of body weight on the back leg. Bend the back knee over the big toe; ensure the front knee is slightly bent.

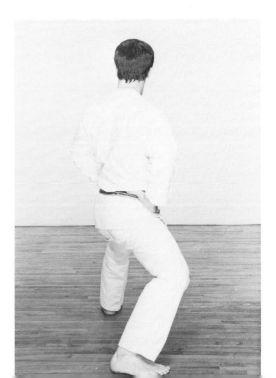

*Turn from position **3**.*
Change stance position and direction by pivoting the hips and transferring weight to the right leg. Right knee is fully bent and positioned over the knee.

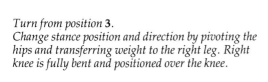

KIBA DACHI (SIDE OR STRADDLE STANCE)

1 *Assume kiba dachi position by placing your feet twice hip-width apart, toes turned in and knees pushed out, weight equally distributed.*

2 *Advance in stance by stepping smoothly across, placing your left foot in front of your right.*

3 *Advance right foot, returning to position shown in picture* **1**.

BOB RHODES

Uke (Blocks)

Bob Rhodes, 5th dan, is a KUGB senior instructor, grading examiner and executive officer. He is a former member of the KUGB British team.

contact than direct. All blocks should deflect attacks safely away from the target area.

With correct body movement and timing one can –

1   Deflect an opponents attack and make an opening for a counter attack.
2   Parry an opponents attack whilst making an evasive movement to a safe position until a chance to counter presents itself.
3   Use such force as to unbalance your opponent and enable you to take advantage of his position.
4   Turn defensive techniques to offensive techniques by applying mainly to leg and arm joints.

In this modern day and age of karate, young karateka train and look to the flair and excitement of championships, which is good in its own right, but let us not forget to work hard and diligently on the techniques that protect our bodies.

Note: in all these basic blocks, the hips are angled at 45° to the left or right from the front, according to the forward leg.

Introduction

Blocking techniques are of vital importance in karate. Practised diligently and executed correctly they can turn your opponent's attack to your advantage.

Most blocking techniques are of an 'arc' movement, and cover, on execution, a large part of the body. The contact part of most blocks is the wrist. The technique should therefore end with a twisting action of the wrist so that there is more of a deflective

GEDAN BARAI (DOWNWARD BLOCK)

1   *Starting position: bring your left foot across to meet the right, bending the knees fully. At the same time extend your right arm straight forward, and pointing slightly down. Bring your left fist up over your right shoulder. Your palm should face your neck.*

2   *Keep your upper body still as you slide your left foot forward and out to the halfway position for zenkutsu dachi.*

3   *Complete zenkutsu dachi, twisting your hips and upper body to 45°. At the same time, bring your left fist down and across your body, twisting your fist palm downwards on completion of the block, stopping it a few inches above your knee as you pull your right fist back to your hip, palm upwards. You must block at the same moment that you twist your hips.*

Application

Bob Rhodes uses gedan barai to block Billy Higgins' chudan mae geri attack.

All blocks are demonstrated by Bob Rhodes, with Billy Higgins

4 *Turn. Extend your left arm straight behind and pointing slightly down, and bring your right fist up over your left shoulder, palm facing your neck. At the same time move your back leg all the way across, so that when you turn your feet will again be shoulder-width apart.*

3a *Side view of position 3.*

5 *Turn by twisting your hips and driving your left leg straight while simultaneously executing the downward block with your right arm and retracting your left arm.*

Gedan barai is used to defend against attacks to the middle or lower body. The fist is brought, from the opposite side of the neck, down and across the body, and the block finishes with the step. It is used throughout the lesson as a starting (or kamae) position for many other techniques.

General

A good stance is essential when blocking. Ensure that your arm techniques are synchronized with your leg and hip movements. You must block at the moment when the hips twist and the back leg locks straight.

31

AGE UKE (RISING BLOCK)

1   *Starting position: bring the left foot across to the right foot as you bend your knees. As you do so straighten your right arm, up and forwards. Position your left fist at your waist.*

2   *Slide your left foot forwards to the halfway zenkutsu dachi position. Keep upper body and arms still.*

3   *Drive forwards into zenkutsu dachi by thrusting the back leg straight. At the same time twist the hips and upper body forwards to 45°: execute the block with the left fist across and above the head whilst retracting the right fist to your right hip.*

This block is used to defend attacks to the head.

3a   *Side view of position* **3**.
Blocking arm is approximately one fist's distance from the front of the head, and above the eyeline at a 45° angle.

Application

Bob Rhodes defends using age uke against Billy Higgins' jodan oi zuki attack. Billy's punch to the head is deflected above and away from his target.

SOTO UDE UKE (OUTSIDE BLOCK)

1 *Starting position: bring the left foot across to the right foot as you fully bend your knees. Extend your right arm straight in front with the hand open and the palm facing down. At the same time, keeping the left fist closed, raise it above and behind the head as shown.*

2 *Slide the left foot forward halfway to zenkutsu dachi. Keep your upper body and arms still.*

3 *Drive forward into zenkutsu dachi by thrusting the back leg straight; twist the hips and upper body forward to 45° and block down and across the front of the body with your left forearm whilst pulling your right fist back to your waist.*

Soto ude uke is a closed-hand block used to deflect an attack. The block starts outside the body area, moving inwards to deflect the attack past the target. It is normally used to chudan, but may be used to jodan.

3a   *Side view of position* **3**. *It is important that the blocking fist is level with the shoulder and the forearm is held at 45°, with the elbow clear of the body.*

Application

Billy Higgins' chudan yoko geri kekomi attack is blocked by Bob Rhodes' soto ude uke. Note how the blow is deflected past the body, while the right hand is poised ready to counter-attack.

UCHE UDE UKE (INSIDE BLOCK)

1 Starting position: bring the left foot across the right foot as you fully bend your knees. Extend your right arm straight in front with the hand open and the palm facing down. Bring the left fist, also palm down, across the body to the waist.

2 Slide the left foot halfway forwards, keeping your weight on your right leg and your upper body and arms still.

3 Drive forwards into zenkutsu dachi by thrusting the back leg straight. At the same time twist the hips and upper body forwards to 45°. Bring the blocking arm across the front of the body to finish in line with the left side of the body.

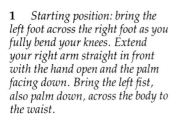

This is another closed-hand block generally used to deflect a blow to the front or side of the body, but it starts and finishes within the target area, moving from the inside outwards. It is occasionally used to block jodan.

3a *Side view of position* **3**. *When blocking chudan it's important that the blocking fist is level with the shoulder and the forearm is held at 45° with the elbow clear of the body.*

Application

Billy Higgins is attacking with jodan mawashi geri. Bob Rhodes is defending with jodan uche ude uke, stopping the kick from reaching its target.

37

SHUTO UKE (KNIFE-HAND BLOCK)

1   *Starting position: place your left foot lightly just in front of your right foot, keeping your hips square. At the same time extend your right arm out straight in front of you, hand open, palm down. Bring your left hand up so that its open palm faces the right side of your neck. It's important to keep your elbow down.*

2   *Slide your left foot further forward and complete kokutsu dachi. Bring the arm across the body to block so that the fingertips finish at shoulder height. Keep the right hand open, and bring it back to protect the solar plexus, palm up.*

2a   *Side view of position* **2**.

Shuto uke is an open-hand technique generally executed in kokutsu dachi. It is important to keep the hand straight and in line with the forearm, with the thumb tucked well in. This can be used to defend against chudan or jodan attacks.

3   *Turn the head and look behind; at the same time raise the right hand up to the left side of your neck, and extend the left arm straight behind, palm down.*

4   *As you complete the turn, the right hand blocks shuto uke while the left hand is pulled back to the solar plexus.*

Application

Billy Higgins' attack, chudan oi zuki, is blocked with shuto uke.

General

With this block, it is very important that the actual blocking area used is the side of the hand, and not the edge of the little finger.

39

ANDY SHERRY 6TH DAN

Tsuki (Punches)

Introduction

As with all karate techniques the punch requires the co-ordinated use of all the body's muscles. The aim is to focus the power of the whole body at the point of impact in order to hit effectively and to develop muscle strength and flexibility.

Although there are many types of punching techniques, in karate the one most widely used is the forefist straight punch, and this is used in this section. The fist must travel in a straight line to the target to be most effective, and control of the position of the elbow is very important. If the elbow swings to the side the punch will shudder from side to side; therefore make sure that the elbow is always directly behind the fist throughout the punch. The punch will shudder up and down if the angle of the elbow is not smoothly co-ordinated with the forward movement of the punch, resulting in the fist being made to travel on a curve either under or over the direct line to the target. The opposite arm should also be retracted on a direct line, again making sure that the elbow does not swing away from the side. The punching arm must be twisted at the very end of the movement; if the arm twists too early it causes the elbow to swing out.

Beginners should practise the punch lightly, concentrating on developing the correct technique. As competence increases, the development of speed and focus becomes more important. The powerful use of muscle must be brought in to propel both arms to maximum speed, and maximum tension must be used upon completing the technique.

The punch must also be practised with the various body movements, such as hip twisting or stepping, etc., together with the various aspects of development that they entail.

Once a high level of technique, speed and focus is reached, the student then starts practising the punch by snapping back to its starting position. But the same line must be maintained and at the point of impact the same focus must be applied as with the thrust punch.

This step by step training structure must be adhered to under a competent instructor if the students are to reach their maximum potential. There are no short cuts in the development of good karate.

CHOKU ZUKI

1 *Standing firmly with the feet at shoulder-width apart and keeping the hips square, extend the left fist to the front. Keep the arm straight and the head up. The right fist is touching the body slightly above the hip, with the palm of the fist facing upwards. Keep the elbow in.*

2 *Twist and pull the left fist back towards the body so that the elbow is in line with the hip, and bring the right fist forward to meet it, but still palm up.*

This is a standard exercise alternating left and right punches to develop technique. It is important to keep your elbows in at every stage.

3 *The right fist moves further forward and the left fist towards the hip.*

4 *Turn the right fist so that it faces down as you straighten your arm. At the same time turn the left fist so that the palm faces up.*

OI ZUKI (STEPPING PUNCH)

1 *Starting position: Assume kamae position shown*

2 *Forcefully pull the right leg forward to meet the left, keeping the knees fully bent. Extend your left arm, do not move the right arm, and allow your body to assume a full square-on position.*

3 *Move the right foot forward and out while keeping weight on left leg, left foot straight and maintain upper body position.*

Oi zuki is a stepping punch which generally uses zenkutsu dachi. The striking hand is on the same side as the leading leg.

All punches are demonstrated by Andy Sherry, with Billy Higgins and Frank Brennan

4 *Drive right leg forward by thrusting left leg straight. Right-fist punch should be co-ordinated with finish of step, as should retraction of left hand. Ensure left foot remains flat.*

Application

Having blocked Billy Higgins' mae geri attack, Andy Sherry counter-attacks with jodan oi zuki.

5 *Side view of position 4.*

KIZAMI ZUKI (JAB OR LEADING-HAND PUNCH)

3   *Side view of* **2**.

1   *Assume kamae position shown.*

2   *Punch with left fist to jodan and retract right fist to the side, whilst rotating the body strongly in the direction of the punch. Ensure that you keep facing straight ahead, that your left knee remains directly over your foot, that your back leg is locked straight, and the foot remains flat.*

Kizami zuki is a punch delivered on the same side as the leading leg. The shoulder and hips are at 45°. It is sometimes known as a lunge punch.

Application

Having blocked an oi zuki attack, Frank Brennan is able to counter-attack effectively from close in with jodan kizami zuki.

GYAKU ZUKI (REVERSE PUNCH)

3   *Side view of 2.*

1   *Assume kamae position shown.*   2   *Simultaneously execute chudan punch, retract opposite fist to side and strongly rotate the body in the direction of the punch. Ensure that you keep facing straight, that your left knee remains directly over your foot, and that your back leg is locked straight and that the foot remains flat.*

Gyaku zuki is a punch delivered from the arm opposite the leading leg, e.g. left leg forward, right arm punches. Generally the stance is maintained whilst the hips are rotated in conjunction with the punch.

Application

Having blocked Billy Higgins' attack, Andy Sherry counter-attacks with a chudan gyaku zuki to the solar plexus.

TERRY O'NEILL

Keri Waza (Kicks)

Terry O'Neill, 5th dan, is a KUGB senior instructor and grading examiner. He is the editor of *Fighting Arts International*, and many times British kata and kumite champion and European and world team champion.

Introduction

The legs are the strongest 'weapons' on the human body. Even on an untrained individual the lower limbs are longer and far more powerful than the upper limbs . . . but in the case of a well-trained karateka, this advantage is multiplied dramatically! Not only is the limiting factor of balance no longer an obstacle – this is one of the first things a novice of the art is taught to overcome – but the precise methods and execution of the many different karate kicks make them potentially lethal – albeit natural – weapons. The kicks are devastatingly effective because they use the full force of the bodyweight, directed through the snap or drive of the foot and knee at a specific target on the opponent's body.

Learning to do this does not come easily – but then nothing worthwhile ever does. A karateka must be able to kick effectively to all points of the compass – to the front and rear, laterally to both sides and indeed in any and every direction from which a possible attack could be made. Because the majority of people do little else with their legs than use them as a means of transport, developing them as effective weapons requires considerably more time and effort than it does to acquire proficiency in hand techniques. Kicking techniques make greater demands on agility, bodily strength, flexibility and stamina than do punches for example.

To reduce the risk of injury to the hips, groin, legs and feet, I would recommend that correct warm-up procedure, including adequate stretching, should precede all kicking practice.

There is no short cut to developing dynamic and effective kicks (or any other karate technique for that matter) . . . The quickest and surest way to developing expertise in the keri waza (kicking techniques) of karate is by regular arduous training. A karateka should follow exactly the principles and direction given by a competent sensei and this, coupled with daily training, is a definite formula for success.

MAE GERI (FRONT KICK)

1 *Assume kamae position shown.*

2 *Keeping the left leg strongly bent, bring the right knee up high in front of the chest. Turn the foot up and curl the toes back to expose the ball of the foot. Ensure you maintain full control of your upper body: do not move your arms.*

3 *Straighten the kicking leg, driving forcefully forward with the hips and striking straight on with the ball of the foot.* **Note:** *the supporting foot is flat on the floor when the kick is being executed.*

Mae geri is a long-reaching, straight kick. It can be used either with a snapping technique (keagi), which is most common, or with a thrusting action (kekomi).

2a *side view of* **2**. **Note:** *a strongly bent left leg is essential for maintaining balance, and helps to keep the hips level prior to execution of the kick.*

Demonstrated by Terry O'Neil

4 *Return to position **2**, keeping the knee up. You must be able to hold this position and remain well-balanced before returning to the floor.*

5 *Step forward into a kamae position, with the right leg forward and simultaneously change your guard position, i.e. right hand forward.*

Application

3a *side view of **3**. The foot must be turned down on impact so that contact is made with the ball and not the heel.*

In this example, Terry exploits the superior reach of the kick to the punch.

51

YOKO GERI KEKOMI (SIDE THRUST KICK)

1 *Starting position: move the right foot to the left foot, and assume kamae position.*

2 *Raise the right knee to a high position. Maintain an upright posture and control your guard. Keep your left knee strongly bent.*

3 *Thrust from the hip and lock the leg in a straight line. As for all thrust kicks, lock your body momentarily. You are striking with the outside edge of your foot.*

This is a kick to the side with the leg locked straight, whilst pivoting and driving the hip in the direction of the kick.

Application

Frank Brennan uses yoko geri kekomi against Jimmy Brennan.

Demonstrated by Frank Brennan

4 *Pull the hips and leg back, making sure to regain balance and upright posture, and facing forward for the change of kicking direction.*

5 *Twist and drive through 90° from the hip, and lock the leg straight out to the front. Do not allow your head to twist away as you kick – you should always be looking in the direction of the kick.*

6 *Pull the hips and legs back powerfully, making sure to regain balance and upright posture.*

7 *Step forward into zenkutsu dachi with the right leg.*

53

YOKO GERI KEAGE (SNAP KICK)

This is a kick to the side, utilizing a snapping motion, and is used at a closer range than yoko geri kekomi.

1 *Starting position: moving the right foot to the left foot and assume kamae position shown.*

2 *Raise the right knee whilst maintaining an upright posture and ensuring both arms remain still.*

Demonstrated by Terry O'Neill

3 *The lower leg snaps upwards in an arc and returns . . .*

4 *. . . while maintaining a high knee position.*

5 *Return to starting position.*

Application

Terry O'Neill blocks and then catches Bob Poynton's gi, then counter-attacks using jodan yoko geri keage.

MAWASHI GERI (ROUNDHOUSE KICK)

This is a powerful kick which utilizes a very big circular motion with a strong twisting of the hip. It travels much further than mae geri. Co-ordination is all-important here. This spectacular kick is very popular in competition.

1 *Adopt a kamae position.*

2 *Raise the right knee and foot to a high position to the side of the body, keeping the ankle turned up and toes curled back. Ensure that the supporting leg remains still and strongly bent. Keep arms still, with hips held back.*

6 *Side view of position **2**.*

Demonstrated by Terry O'Neill

3 *Without dropping the knee, combine the strong twist of the hip with the full pivot of the left leg, and co-ordinate all with the kick.*

4 *Keep the knee in a high position and snap the lower leg fully back.*

5 *Step forward with the right leg into zenkutsu dachi.*

7 *Side view of position **3**.*

Application

Terry O'Neill evades Bob Poynton's mae geri and counters with jodan mawashi geri.

USHIRO GERI (REVERSE THRUST KICK)

Ushiro geri is one of the most (if not *the* most) powerful kicks within karate. It utilizes a spinning and thrusting action of the hips. Great speed, co-ordination, timing and accuracy are essential for success.

1   *Assume kamae position shown.*

2   *Raise the right knee without moving the upper body, arms or supporting leg.*

Demonstrated by Frank Brennan

3 *Spin the hips quickly through 180° and the hips and kicking leg are driven powerfully in the direction of the target. The emphasis is on striking with the heel, for which reason the foot should be held tightly back. At this point your body should be locked with maximum focus.*

4 *Pull the kicking leg and hips powerfully back to control stability before moving in.*

5 *Step forward into zenkutsu dachi.*

Application

Frank Brennan quickly spins and attacks with ushiro geri before his opponent, Jimmy Brennan, even has time to react.

BOB POYNTON

Uchi Waza (Strikes)

Introduction

Usually the mere mention of the word karate is enough to evoke a cry of chop-chop, followed by an open handed swipe to an imaginary neck, from those unfamiliar with the do or way of karate. Indeed my first conception of karate stemmed from a visit to the cinema where I saw an Oriental Master by the name of 'Odd Job' (in real life Harold Sakata) dispatch several opponents with the same deadly chop. In reality this technique (shuto uchi) is not one of the most commonly used, yet in a way it epitomizes the principle behind karate, that is, to concentrate one's maximum power over a small area to a vulnerable point. This principle can equally apply to the use of the knuckles (as in uraken), point of the elbow (empi), finger tips (nukite), the inside ridge of the hand (haito) and bottom of the fist (tettsui). There are other strikes which are used, but usually not until beyond black belt level.

This term 'strike' in karate is generally used to denote a hand technique other than punching, catching or blocking: As in the case with punching and blocking a selection of stances can be used for maximum power and stability and to vary distances whilst striking. Certain strikes will by their nature lend themselves to particular stances and will therefore be commonly used during practice sessions, but as with all techniques it is advantageous to experiment and develop using a variety of strike/stance combinations. Like all karate attacks, the effectiveness of a particular strike technique will depend not just on how but on where it is delivered. The elbow is a naturally strong weapon and can be used to any accessible weak point. Other striking techniques need to be delivered to carefully chosen targets. For example, nukite to a developed abdomen would result in damage to the attacker's fingers, so it is generally used against throat and eyes. In practice it is wise not to aim attacks to the eyes for very obvious safety reasons, and even in self-defence situations it is not acceptable unless there is a very serious threat.

All strikes demonstrated by Bob Poynton and Jimmy Poynton (3rd dan)

SHUTO UCHI (KNIFE HAND STRIKE)

Preparation

1 Take the right hand up with hand open and finger tips close to the ear, palm facing up and forward. The opposite arm should be extended forward at stomach height. Rotate body away from direction of strike.

Strike

2 Simultaneously, rotate body, strike and retract opposite hand to the side. The striking hand should travel in an arc away from its starting position then back in towards the target. As target is reached, the hand should be twisted so the palm is fully up and arm locked straight.

Application

3 The defender blocks the attacker's kick in such a way as to pull him onto the counter-attack.

4 The counter-attack is delivered to the front side of the neck as the attacker lands . . .

HAITO UCHI (RIDGE HAND STRIKE)

Preparation

1   *Take the right hand to the waist with hand closed and palm up. Extend opposite arm forward to stomach height. Rotate body away from direction of strike.*

Strike

2   *Simultaneously rotate body, strike and retract opposite hand to the side. The striking hand should travel in an arc away from its starting position then back in towards the target. As target is reached the hand should be opened and twisted so palm is fully down and arm locked straight.*

Application

3   *The defender deflects the attack in such a way that a clear path is opened up for the strike to follow.*

4   *The counter strike is delivered immediately to the temple area, not allowing the attacker to recover his guard.*

URAKEN UCHI (BACK FIST STRIKE)

Preparation

1　*Bring the right hand up with fist closed and palm touching the neck. The elbow should be chin height and in the centre. The opposite arm is extended at shoulder height.*

Strike

2　*Simultaneously rotate body, strike and retract the opposite hand to the side. The strike should travel straight to the target with the elbow held still and acting as a pivot for the forearm. The hand should twist as the arm straightens so as to strike with the two major knuckles.*

3　*This is a snapping technique and so the striking hand should be pulled back immediately to near side of the chest. Again elbow should remain still and act as a pivot.*

Application

4 (right)　*As the defender blocks the attacker's punch he simultaneously delivers a counter-attack to side of head using uraken uchi.*

NUKITE (SPEAR HAND)

Strike

2 *Simultaneously rotate body, strike and retract the opposite hand to the side. As target is reached the striking hand should be open with arm and fingers extended for maximum reach and penetration. The hand should be twisted with palm facing either inside or down depending on the accessibility of target.*

Preparation

1 *Take the right hand to the waist with hand closed and palm up. Extend the opposite arm forward to stomach height and rotate body away from the direction of the attack.*

Application

3 (below) *In this case the palm of the striking hand is facing down to allow maximum penetration to the throat.*

TETTSUI UCHI (BOTTOM FIST STRIKE)

Preparation

1 *Bring the right fist above and behind the head with palm out. The elbow should be held right back. Extend the opposite arm forward and rotate body away from the direction of attack.*

Attack

2 *Simultaneously rotate body, strike and retract the opposite hand to the side. The attacking fist in this example travels over and down to strike target from above, but this strike can also be delivered from the side, or from under. In all cases this strike is delivered using the bottom of the fist. The arm should finish slightly bent and the bottom of the fist held relevant to the target area, for example, the bridge of the nose, the collar bone, cheek bone, kidneys or groin etc.*

Application

3 *In this example the attacker strikes down to the bridge of the defender's nose. Note that arm is slightly bent to aid control.*

YOKO EMPI UCHI (SIDE ELBOW STRIKE)

Preparation

1 *Stretch the attacking arm across the face with hand open and palm up. Stretch the opposite arm across the chest with hand open and palm down.*

Attack

2 *Drive the attacking elbow sideways and down and simultaneously pull the opposite hand to the side. The strike should be made with the point of the elbow. As elbow lands the fist should be twisted palm down and locked on to near side of the chest.*

Application

3 *The defender has turned his body sideways both to avoid the attack and to facilitate the application of the side elbow strike. His opposite arm is used in this case to pull his attacker on to his elbow.*

AGE EMPI UCHI (RISING ELBOW STRIKE)

Application

3   *After blocking the attack, the defender uses his opposite hand to pull his opponent on to the counter.*

Preparation

1   *Take the hand of attacking arm to the waist, with fist closed and palm up. Stretch the opposite arm up and to the side of the head. Rotate body slightly away from the direction of attack.*

Attack

2   *Simultaneously rotate body, strike and retract the opposite hand to the side. The attacking elbow should travel straight to the target and remain close to body en route. Finish with attacking elbow as high as possible, with fist closed and palm touching the neck.*

MAWASHI EMPI UCHI (ROUND ELBOW STRIKE)

Preparation

1 *Take hand of attacking arm to the waist with palm facing up. Extend the opposite arm forward at stomach height. Rotate body away from the direction of attack.*

Attack

2 *Simultaneously rotate body, strike and retract opposite hand to the side. Take fist of attacking arm directly up to the near side of chest and drive elbow forward and round. As elbow reaches the target the fist should be twisted palm down and locked to the chest.*

Application

3 *The defender steps in and simultaneously deflects attacker's punch and drives his elbow round into the attacker's chest.*

OTOSHI EMPI UCHI (DOWNWARD ELBOW STRIKE)

Preparation

1 *The right arm is stretched up by the side of the head with palm facing forward or inside. The opposite arm is stretched down and body slightly rotated away from the front.*

Attack

2 *Simultaneously rotate body, strike down and pull the opposite hand to the side. The attacking forearm should finish in a vertical position and fist should stop at shoulder height. The palm can face inside, as shown, or towards the body.*

Application

3 *Having pulled the attacker off balance, the
defender attacks down to his opponent's spine or
neck. Notice how body is kept upright when
counter-attacking in order to maintain balance.*

BILLY HIGGINS

Ashi Barai (Sweeps)

Billy Higgins, 5th dan, is a senior KUGB instructor and grading examiner. He is a former British and European kumite champion and member of the former British world championship team.

Introduction

The legs can be used to disturb the balance of or to throw an opponent – this is generally referred to as a sweep. When practising with an opponent, maximum control should be used in the early stages of learning and developing sweeps. The emphasis should be on accuracy and good timing. Under no circumstances should an attack be made to the knees.

Sweeps can be used in many ways for attacking or counter-attacking one or both legs together of the opponent. They can be applied with the sole of the foot, the instep, or even the calf. Weight distribution plays a very important parts in these techniques, both on the part of the person performing the sweep and by the opponent.

ASHI BARAI (FOOT SWEEP)   Demonstrated by Billy Higgins

1   *Assume kamae position.*

2   *Transfer your weight completely on to your front leg. Take your sweeping leg forward, keeping your foot as close to the floor as possible. The hips should stay back and the body remain upright.*

3   *Carry the sweeping leg through in a controlled manner to a point past the supporting leg.*

4   *Step forward into stance.*

ASHI BARAI followed by OI ZUKI

Demonstrated by Billy Higgins and Jim Murphy (2nd dan)

1 *Execute ashi barai. Note that the attack is delivered as low as possible for maximum effectiveness. Do not twist hips but drive body weight forward and sweeping foot across.*

2 *The attack (oi zuki) has to be delivered immediately whilst the opponent is off balance and in a weak position.*

ASHI BARAI, follow down with GYAKU ZUKI

1 *Execute ashi barai and now twist hips in direction of sweep so that maximum body weight is applied to sweep. The sweeping leg is taken through to the point where recovery of balance for the opponent is impossible.*

2 *As the opponent is landing, and thus at his most vulnerable, the counter-attack is delivered. Position body directly over fallen opponent and drive body weight down with punch for maximum effectiveness.*

Kata (Prearranged Forms)

Frank Brennan, 4th dan, is grading examiner, member of KUGB British team and current all-style British and European champion.

Introduction

Kata, said by many masters to be the soul of karate-do, are the very foundation and must be practised diligently by both student and master alike. As with all aspects of karate training, the co-ordination of body and mind is of paramount importance. When the karateka is performing a kata they must strive for technical perfection. The movements must be performed at the correct speed and with a smooth action, finishing with good focus. You must also ensure that the correct timing and rhythm are maintained. The whole kata must contain one hundred per cent concentration, maximum effort and be performed with zanshin, the state of total awareness and martial spirit.

Kata training by its very nature offers many benefits to its practitioner. A wide variety of techniques are learned – blocks, strikes, kicks and stances, along with an understanding of body shifting, balance and co-ordination. It must always be stressed that karate kata and technique can only be performed in an advanced manner after many years of training, when all the above aspects have been developed then co-ordinated to make the movements effective.

Kata training like all aspects of karate training is very demanding, but one must always use one's self discipline to overcome these barriers in an effort to strive for perfection of one's technique and character. Only then can you start to understand the true meaning of karate-do.

KIHON KATA (BASIC FORMS)

Demonstrated by Billy Higgins

1   *Assume kamae position shown.*

2   *Turn and step with left leg and block gedan barai to the left.*

3   *Step with right leg and punch chudan oi zuki.*

7   *Look to front; step with left leg and prepare arms for gedan barai . . .*

8   *. . . twist hips, lock stance and block gedan barai.*

9   *Step forward with right leg and punch chudan oi zuki.*

4 *Move right foot diagonally behind and prepare arms for gedan barai . . .*

5 *. . . complete stance with strong hip twist and block gedan barai.*

6 *Step with left foot and punch chudan oi zuki.*

10 *Step forward with left leg and punch chudan oi zuki.*

11 *Step forward with right leg and punch chudan oi zuki with* **KIAI**.

12 *Step behind with left leg and prepare arms for gedan barai . . .*

13 . . . *execute gedan barai with hip twist.*

14 *Step forward with right leg and punch chudan oi zuki.*

15 *Step behind with right leg and prepare hands for gedan barai . . .*

19 . . . *execute gedan barai with hip twist.*

20 *Step forward with right leg and make chudan oi zuki.*

21 *Step forward with left leg and make chudan oi zuki.*

80

16 . . . *twist hips and execute gedan barai.*

17 *Step forward with left leg and punch chudan oi zuki.*

18 *Step to the left side and prepare arms for gedan barai . . .*

22 *Step forward with right leg and make chudan oi zuki with* **KIAI**.

23 *Step behind with left leg and position arms for gedan barai . . .*

24 . . . *execute gedan barai with hip twist.*

81

25 *Step forward with right leg and punch chudan oi zuki.*

26 *Step behind with right leg and prepare arms for gedan barai . . .*

27 *. . . execute gedan barai with hip twist.*

28 *Step forward with left leg and punch chudan oi zuki.*

29 *Move left leg back to starting position.*

HEIAN SHODAN

1 *Assume kamae position shown.*

2 *Step with left leg and block gedan barai.*

3 *Step with right leg and punch chudan oi zuki.*

4 *Move right foot diagonally behind and prepare arms for gedan barai . . .*

5 *. . . complete stance with strong hip twist and block gedan barai.*

6 *Withdraw right leg diagonally back towards left leg to halfway, and simultaneously pull right arm back above head in preparation for tettsui uchi . . .*

7 . . . *without stepping, rotate upper body and strike down with tettsui uchi.*

8 *Step with left foot and punch chudan oi zuki.*

9 *Look to front; step with left leg and prepare arms for gedan barai . . .*

13 *Step forward with right leg and block jodan age uke with* **KIAI**.

14 *Step behind to halfway position, and prepare arms for gedan barai . . .*

15 . . . *execute gedan barai with hip twist.*

10   *. . . twist hips, lock stance and block gedan barai.*

11   *Step forward with right leg and block jodan age uke.*

12   *Step forward with left leg and block jodan age uke.*

16   *Step forward with right leg and punch chudan oi zuki.*

17   *Step behind with right leg and prepare arms for gedan barai . . .*

18   *. . . twist hips and execute gedan barai.*

19   *Step forward with left leg and punch chudan oi zuki.*

20   *Step to the left side and prepare hands for gedan barai . . .*

21   *. . . execute gedan barai with hip twist.*

25   *Step behind with left leg and position arms for shuto uke . . .*

26   *. . . execute shuto uke with hip twist.*

27   *Make three-quarters step with right foot and prepare arms for shuto uke . . .*

22 *Step forward with right leg and make chudan oi zuki.*

23 *Step forward with left leg and make chudan oi zuki.*

24 *Step forward with right leg and make chudan oi zuki with* **KIAI**.

28 *. . . step diagonally and execute shuto uke.*

29 *Step across with right leg and prepare arms for shuto uke . . .*

30 *. . . twist hips and execute shuto uke.*

31   *Step three quarters with left leg and prepare arms for shuto uke . . .*

32   *. . . step diagonally with left leg; twist body and block with shuto uke.*

33   *Move left leg back to starting position.*

HEIAN NIDAN

Demonstrated by Bob Rhodes

1 *Assume kamae position shown.*

2 *Step with left leg and take both arms down to right side . . .*

3 *. . . complete stance with body twist and execute jodan block.*

4 *Taking care not to move stance, rotate top half of body anti-clockwise and simultaneously punch to stomach with right hand (ura zuki) and block with left hand jodan nagashi uke . . .*

5 *. . . immediately rotate body clockwise and punch chudan choku zuki with left hand, retracting right hand to side.*

6 *Without moving stance face behind and take both arms down to left side, fists closed, palms facing behind . . .*

7 . . . *rotate hips, change stance and block to right side jodan.*

8 *Taking care not to move stance, rotate upper body clockwise and punch chudan ura zuki, simultaneously blocking with right hand jodan nagashi uke* . . .

9 . . . *immediately twist upper body anti-clockwise, punch with right hand to chudan, and pull left hand back to side.*

13 *Snap back right fist to chest and right foot to your supporting knee* . . .

14 . . . *turn and face to the front, and prepare arms for shuto uke* . . .

15 . . . *step back with right leg into kokutsu dachi, blocking shuto uke as you land.*

10   *Move left foot halfway forward under body and start to face right side . . .*

11   *. . . pull back right foot to left, place right fist on top of left fist with right palm towards body, and turn head fully to face right . . .*

12   *. . . simultaneously execute jodan yoko geri keage (side snap kick) and uraken uke (back fist block).*

16   *Step forward with right leg and make chudan shuto uke.*

17   *Step forward with left leg and make chudan shuto uke.*

18   *Bring right foot to meet the left and simultaneously block chudan osae uke . . .*

19 . . . *step forward with right leg into zenkutsu dachi and attack with right hand chudan nukite.* **KIAI**. *Keep left hand under right elbow for support.*

20 *Step across with left leg and prepare hands for shuto uke . . .*

21 . . . *twist into stance and execute shuto uke.*

25 . . . *twist into stance and execute shuto uke.*

26 *Step three quarters with left leg, prepare arms for shuto uke and face to the side . . .*

27 . . . *step into stance and execute shuto uke with strong hip twist.*

22 *Make three-quarter step with right leg, keeping body still and preparing arms for shuto uke . . .*

23 *. . . twist hips and execute shuto uke.*

24 *Step across with right leg, turn head and prepare arms for shuto uke . . .*

28 *Step across with left leg, bringing hips square and crossing arms in preparation for chudan uchi uke . . .*

29 *. . . push right side of chest forward, pulling left leg slightly back. Simultaneously block chudan uchi uke with right arm, and pull back left arm to side.*

30 *Taking care not to move arms, kick jodan mae geri with right leg . . .*

31 . . . *step forward with right leg and on landing punch chudan gyaku zuki, pulling opposite hand back to side.*

32 *Prepare arms for left chudan uchi uke . . .*

33 . . . *simultaneously rotate body, block and pull front foot slightly back.*

37 . . . *step forward with right leg into zenkutsu dachi and block chudan morote uke. The left hand supports the right elbow.*

38 *Step across with left leg to face right, and block gedan barai.*

39 *Step three quarters with right leg, keeping right hand by side, and stretch left arm diagonally upwards . . .*

34 Kick with left leg jodan mae geri, taking care not to move arms . . .

35 . . . step forward with left leg and punch chudan gyaku zuki with right arm as you land, pulling opposite hand back to side.

36 Bring right foot forward, to left, and cross both arms down and behind with arms relaxed, fists closed and palms pointing inside . . .

40 . . . step forward with right leg and twist body, blocking age uke.

41 Step across with your right leg to face right and block gedan barai.

42 Step three quarters with left leg, keeping left hand by side, and stretching right arm diagonally up.

43   *Step and twist into stance and block age uke with* **KIAI**.

44   *Step back with left leg to starting position.*

HEIAN SANDAN

Demonstrated by Bob Rhodes

1   *Assume kamae position.*

2   *Step to the left side with left leg into kokutsu dachi and block chudan uchi uke.*

3   *Take right foot forward and cross arms with left palm touching neck and right arm straight across body . . .*

4   *. . . lock knees straight, simultaneously executing gedan barai with your left arm and chudan uchi uke with your right.*

5   *Maintaining stance and body position, take right fist up with palm facing neck, and swing left arm across body . . .*

6   *. . . simultaneously block gedan barai with your right arm and chudan uchi uke with your left arm.*

7   *Step behind with right leg into kokutsu dachi and execute chudan uchi uke.*

8   *Step forward with your left leg. Take your right fist up with your palm facing your neck. Take your left arm across your body . . .*

9   *. . . simultaneously lock your knees whilst blocking gedan barai with your right arm and uchi uke with your left arm.*

13   *. . . complete kokutsu dachi with hip twist and block morote uke, using your right fist to support your left elbow.*

14   *Step forward with your right leg and simultaneously block down osae uke with your left hand . . .*

15   *. . . complete movement into zenkutsu dachi and attack chudan nukite with opposite hand under and supporting the elbow.*

10   *Without moving your stance take your left fist to your neck and swing your right arm across your body . . .*

11   *. . . simultaneously block gedan barai with your left arm and uchi uke with your right.*

12   *Step to the front with your left leg, and face to the front taking both arms straight down to your back hip, palms facing inside . . .*

16   *Move left foot to right with half-body turn anti-clockwise, simultaneously twisting right arm anti-clockwise and down . . .*

17   *. . . continue turn into kiba dachi, striking with left hand chudan tettsui, retracting opposite hand to side.*

18   *Step forward with right leg and make chudan oi zuki with* **KIAI**.

19   S-l-o-w-l-y and smoothly pull left foot to right, turning the hips anti-clockwise to face behind. Knees should be straight on completion of turn. Whilst turning, keep left hand at side and bring elbow out whilst taking right hand back to side with elbow also out.

20   Take right foot up and across body to jodan height without moving arms . . .

21   . . . stamp fumikomi strongly with right foot into kiba dachi position, simultaneously blocking empi uke (elbow block).

25   . . . stamp fumikomi strongly with left foot into kiba dachi position, simultaneously blocking empi uke.

26   Attack over the top with jodan uraken uchi . . .

27   . . . snapping the hand immediately back to the side.

22   *Attack over the top with jodan uraken uchi . . .*

23   *. . . snapping the hand immediately back to the side.*

24   *Take left foot up and across body to jodan height without moving arms . . .*

28   *Take right foot up and across body to jodan height without moving arms . . .*

29   *. . . stamp fumikomi strongly with right foot into kiba dachi position, simultaneously blocking empi uke.*

30   *Attack over the top with jodan uraken uchi . . .*

101

31 . . . *snapping the hand immediately back to the side.*

32 *Take right hand diagonally out with arm straight and hand held palm forward . . .*

33 . . . *block with right hand chudan tate shuto uke and simultaneously pull left elbow in.*

37 . . . *twist into kiba dachi facing front and simultaneously attack behind with oshiro empi uchi (left elbow) and jodan zuki.*

38 *Thrust into kiba dachi and simultaneously attack with right ushiro empi uchi and left jodan zuki.* **KIAI**.

39 *Step with right leg back to starting position.*

34   *Step forward with left leg and attack chudan oi zuki.*

35   *Take right foot forward in line with left foot, keeping knees bent, body square and arms still . . .*

36   *. . . stretch across with left leg . . .*

HEIAN YONDAN
Demonstrated by Frank Brennan

1 *Assume kamae position shown.*

2 *Step to the left side in kokutsu dachi and quickly block with the palms of both hands to cover right side . . .*

3 *. . . s-l-o-w-l-y and smoothly take hands around and up to cover face, keeping arms relaxed until the end of the movement, at which point focus very strongly.*

7 *Step forward with right leg into kokutsu dachi, blocking chudan morote uke.*

8 *Step forward with left foot to right foot, keeping knees strongly bent, simultaneously facing to left and pulling both hands to right side (right hand resting above hip, palm up, left hand on top of right hand, palm towards body) . . .*

9 *. . . raise left knee until left foot is level with right knee. Point knee outside; simultaneously take left elbow out to side and take left fist three quarters across chest . . .*

4 *Face right side and block down to cover left side . . .*

5 *. . . s-l-o-w-l-y and smoothly take hands around and up to cover face, keeping arms relaxed until the end of the movement, at which point focus very strongly.*

6 *Step to the front with left leg and simultaneously block down with your left arm gedan barai and your right punching gedan tate zuki. The hands should pass close to the top right of the chest and finish with both wrists adjacent.*

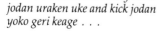  

10 *. . . simultaneously block jodan uraken uke and kick jodan yoko geri keage . . .*

11 *. . . half-snap back leg and arm . . .*

12 *. . . step down with left leg straight and keeping right leg bent, and reach out with left arm straight. Keep right hand at side . . .*

13 . . . *strongly twist hip into zenkutsu dachi, pull back strongly left hand and attack strongly to palm of left hand with right mawashi empi uchi.*

14 *Pull right foot to left, look to right and take both hands to left side (left under, right above) . . .*

15 . . . *raise right knee to side, foot touching left knee, and simultaneously take right hand three quarters of the way across chest . . .*

19 . . . *twist hip strongly into zenkutsu dachi, pulling right hand strongly back and attacking with left elbow to palm of right hand.*

20 *Look to left side and block with gedan shuto uke, bringing right hand to the right side of the head in preparation for striking . . .*

21 . . . *twist hip strongly and rotate stance whilst simultaneously blocking with left hand jodan age shuto uke and striking with shuto uchi to the temple.*

16   . . . *kick jodan yoko geri keage with right leg and block jodan uraken uke . . .*

17   . . . *snap back arm and leg to halfway position . . .*

18   . . . *step down with right leg straight, keeping left leg bent, and reach out with right arm straight . . .*

22   *Kick jodan mae geri with right leg, keeping hands in the same position . . .*

23   . . . *block with left hand chudan osae uke and prepare right hand for striking uraken uchi . . .*

24   . . . *stamp fumikomi with right foot and simultaneously strike with uraken uchi from jodan through to chudan, immediately continuing forward with the left leg tucked behind the right leg.* **KIAI**.

25   *Turn anti-clockwise into kokutsu dachi, and cross fists in front of face with elbows in and palms towards the face (right hand closest to face) . . .*

26   *. . . lock down into stance whilst pulling forearms to the outer side of the body.*

27   *Kick chudan mae geri with right leg without moving arms . . .*

31   *. . . lock down into stance whilst pulling forearms to the outer side of the body (kake uke).*

32   *Kick with left chudan mae geri . . .*

33   *. . . snap leg back and step forward with left chudan oi zuki . . .*

28 . . . *snap leg back and step forward with the right leg and attack chudan oi zuki* . . .

29 . . . *punch with left chudan gyaku zuki.*

30 *Step diagonally to the right into kokutsu dachi and cross both hands in front of face, with left hand closest to face* . . .

34 . . . *punch with right chudan gyaku zuki.*

35 *Step across with left leg into kokutsu dachi and block chudan morote uke.*

36 *Side view of* **35**.

37   *Step forward with right leg into kokutsu dachi and block chudan morote uke.*

38   *Step forward with left leg into kokutsu dachi and block chudan morote uke.*

39   *Step across with left leg, thrust right leg straight and thrust both arms out straight to head height (approximately head-width apart).*

43   *Step forward with right leg into kokutsu dachi and block shuto uke.*

44   *Step back into starting position.*

40   *Bring right knee strongly up to attack with hiza geri (knee attack), simultaneously pulling down strongly with both arms, fists clenched.* **KIAI** . . .

41   *. . . half turn body, look behind and prepare hands for shuto uke . . .*

42   *. . . step back with right leg into kokutsu dachi and block chudan shuto uke.*

HEIAN GODAN

Demonstrated by Bob Poynton

1   *Assume kamae position.*

2   *Step into left side kokutsu dachi and block chudan uchi uke.*

3   *Without altering the stance, twist the upper body and attack with chudan choku zuki.*

7   *S-l-o-w-l-y slide left leg to right, whilst s-l-o-w-l-y turning and facing the front, and s-l-o-w-l-y punching kagi zuki with the right hand.*

8   *Step forward with the right leg into kokutsu dachi and block chudan morote uke.*

9   *Step forward feet together and take both hands horizontally back to the back hip . . .*

4 S-l-o-w-l-y slide the right foot back to the left foot, whilst s-l-o-w-l-y turning and facing the right side and s-l-o-w-l-y punching kagi zuki.

5 Step with right leg into kokutsu dachi and block with right hand chudan uchi uke.

6 Without altering stance, twist upper body and punch chudan choku zuki.

10 . . . step forward with the left leg into zenkutsu dachi and block gedan barai with left hand and simultaneously punch gedan tate zuki with right hand.

11 Take both hands back to sternum with palms in, fists closed . . .

12 . . . thrust both hands up, open them, and block juji uke (x block) whilst simultaneously sliding front foot back and thrusting body weight upwards.

113

13   Step forward, feet together and simultaneously block osae uke with the back of right hand using the palm of the left hand for increased leverage . . .

14   . . . stretch out with right leg, keeping weight on left leg and simultaneously pushing forward with the left fist and locking right fist back to your side . . .

15   . . . step forward with right leg and attack chudan oi zuki. **KIAI**.

19   Look to left and cross left arm under right, hand open and palm down, and cross right arm across body, fist closed . . .

20   . . . s-l-o-w-l-y bring left arm out and across to block with the back of the hand (haishu uke) whilst pulling the right hand s-l-o-w-l-y back to the side.

21   Keeping both hands perfectly still, attack to the palm of the hand with mika zuki geri (crescent kick), twisting the hips through 90° . . .

16   *Turn body anti-clockwise and raise right foot to head height whilst bringing right fist to the neck and extending left arm down . . .*

17   *. . . stamp with right leg fumikomi and simultaneously block gedan barai.*

18   *Side view of **17**.*

22   *. . . twist the hips through a further 90°, step into kiba dachi and attack the palm of the left hand with chudan mawashi empi uchi.*

23   *Twist the hips strongly clockwise, pivot on right foot and pull the left foot behind the right. Simultaneously block morote uke.*

24   *Thrust both right leg and right arm straight, driving the right fist up. At the same time look behind and step lightly out with the left foot.*

25 *Take arms down and up and, as you lift arms, throw right knee strongly up.*

26 *Continue with left knee forcefully up to jump high.*

27 *. . . land with both feet at the same time, with back kept straight and the left foot slightly behind and in line with right foot. Land strongly, simultaneously block down with gedan juji uke.* **KIAI.**

31 *. . . pull left leg strongly across to make kokutsu dachi, and block gedan barai with left hand. Use right hand to balance the left by pulling it back strongly to jodan.*

32 *Slide left foot s-l-o-w-l-y back to the right foot and turn it so that both feet are parallel. Finish the action with the knees straight.*

33 *Rotate the body anti-clockwise, step in with right leg and take right hand down and left hand up ready to block and attack. Both hands should now be open . . .*

28 *Step to the right and up with right leg into zenkutsu dachi, blocking morote uke.*

29 *Move left leg across and bring left arm down straight and right arm up with hand close to the neck. Face front. Note both hands are now open . . .*

30 *. . . twist hips strongly into front stance and simultaneously block with left hand jodan nagashi uke, and attack right hand gedan nukite . . .*

34 *. . . drive hips in and block jodan nagashi uke with right, and attack gedan nukite with the left.*

35 *Pull right leg strongly across into kokutsu dachi, blocking gedan barai with right hand and using left hand to balance the right by pulling it back to jodan.*

36 *Step back to starting position.*

TEKKI SHODAN

Demonstrated by Frank Brennan

1   *Natural stance.*

2   *Assume starting position by moving right foot to left foot with knees straight, hands open and place left hand over right.*

3   *Look sharply to the right and cross left foot over right foot, taking weight on to right leg.*

7   *Sharply turn head to the left and pull both hands strongly down to the right side with right hand palm up and left hand on top, palm facing body.*

8   *Using left hand only, block gedan barai.*

9   *Attack chudan kagi zuki with right hand and pull left fist directly back to the left side.*

5   . . . *stamp fumikomi into kiba dachi, at the same time blocking haishu uke while pulling the left hand strongly back to the side.*

6   *Without moving the stance, twist the upper body to the maximum and attack the palm of the right hand with left mawashi empi uchi.*

4   *Bring right foot straight up to jodan and cross arms in front of body with hands open and right arm under . . .*

10   *S-l-o-w-l-y transfer weight to left leg, stepping across with right leg in front . . .*

11   . . . *transfer weight to right leg and quickly swing left leg to jodan, and take right fist to left shoulder with the palm of the hand facing down.*

12   *Stamp fumikomi into kiba dachi, simultaneously block with right chudan uchi uke and sharply turn head to the front.*

119

13 *Bring left arm in front of right arm in preparation for block . . .*

14 *. . . use left arm to block jodan nagashi uke (sweeping block) and simultaneously punch forward with right hand to balance the block . . .*

15 *. . . take left fist straight forward to attack jodan ura zuki (closed punch), keeping the elbow close to the body. Pull right fist back under left elbow to provide support.*

19 *Look sharply to the right.*

20 *Block with right leg nami ashi, keeping hands and head in the same position . . .*

21 *. . . land in kiba dachi and block chudan soto ude uke, supporting left elbow with right fist.*

16   *Look sharply to the left.*

17   *Block with left leg nami ashi (sweeping block with leg), keeping hands and head in the same position . . .*

18   *. . . land in kiba dachi and simultaneously block with left forearm, supporting blocking elbow with right fist.*

22   *Look sharply left and pull hands strongly to right side.*

23   *Attack with right hand kagi zuki and at the same time with left arm chudan choku zuki.* **KIAI**.

24   *Cross arms in front of chest with left arm underneath, hand open, right arm on top, fist closed . . .*

121

25 . . . s-l-o-w-l-y block haishu uke with left hand, pulling right hand s-l-o-w-l-y to the right side.

26 Attack mawashi empi uchi to palm of left hand.

27 Look sharply to the right and pull hands to left side.

32 . . . stamp fumikomi into kiba dachi, block uchi uke with left arm as you turn head sharply to the front.

33 Bring right arm forward in front of left in preparation to block . . .

31 . . . transfer weight to left leg and immediately swing right leg to jodan, and take left fist to right shoulder with the palm facing down . . .

28 Block gedan barai, using right arm only.

29 Punch kagi zuki with left fist, pulling right hand directly back to side.

30 S-l-o-w-l-y transfer weight to right leg, stepping across with left foot in front of right . . .

34 . . . block jodan nagashi uke with right arm and thrust left arm forward to balance the block . . .

35 . . . attack jodan ura zuki with right fist and use left fist to support right elbow.

36 Look sharply to the right.

123

37 *Block nami ashi with right foot, keeping arms and head in the same position . . .*

38 *. . . land in kiba dachi and block with right forearm supporting blocking elbow with left fist.*

39 *Look sharply to the left.*

43 *Punch chudan kagi zuki with left and chudan choku zuki with right, and* **KIAI**.

44 *Step s-l-o-w-l-y with right foot to left, knees straight, and take hands together with left hand over right, both hands open.*

45 *Step out with right leg to natural stance.*

40 *Block nami ashi with left foot, keeping arms and head in the same position . . .*

41 *. . . land in kiba dachi and block chudan soto ude uke, using left fist to support right elbow.*

42 *Look sharply to the right and pull hands strongly to the left side.*

BASSAI DAI   **Demonstrated by Bob Poynton**

1   *Natural stance.*

2   *Bring right foot to left with knees straight and hands together; left hand is wrapped around the right fist.*

3   *Bring right knee up high and take hands still together, to left side . . .*

7   *Cross arms in preparation for right arm uche uke and take your body square . . .*

8   *. . . block uchi uke with right arm and simultaneously rotate body anti-clockwise, slightly withdrawing from foot to facilitate body action.*

9   *Look behind, raise left arm and stretch out right arm in preparation for soto ude uke while stepping across with right leg . . .*

126

4 . . . *stamp fumikomi into zenkutsu dachi with right foot and attack chudan uraken uchi. Immediately take your weight to the front leg by pulling left leg forward and behind right leg.*

5 *Look behind and step out with left leg, crossing arms in preparation for chudan uche uke* . . .

6 . . . *complete stance, twist hips and block chudan uchi uke.*

10 . . . *twist into stance, blocking soto ude uke with left arm and pulling right hand back to side.*

11 *Cross arms in front of chest with left arm straight and right arm under, fists closed and palms pointing down* . . .

12 . . . *block chudan uchi uke with right arm, pulling left hand back to your side and twisting hips.*

127

13 *Twist to side and pull back right foot, block gedan barai with right arm and bend knees strongly to take you low . . .*

14 *. . . lift right arm up to the side and simultaneously thrust your left hand out and your body up . . .*

15 *. . . step forward with right leg and block with right hand chudan soto ude uke.*

19 *S-l-o-w-l-y block with left hand tate shuto uke by taking your hand forward and across.*

20 *Punch choku zuki with right hand and pull left hand to side.*

21 *Take right fist in front of and just below left shoulder with palm facing down . . .*

16 *Cross arms in front of chest and turn your body square . . .*

17 *. . . block with your left arm chudan uche uke and simultaneously rotate your body, pulling your front leg slightly back to facilitate this movement. Pull your right hand strongly back to your side.*

18 *S-l-o-w-l-y take your left foot back so feet are in line and shoulder-width apart, knees straight, and place left hand on top of right with the palm of the left hand turned towards your body.*

22 *. . . bend left knee, lock right knee and twist hips to make a short zenkutsu dachi as you block right uchi uke.*

23 *Twist back to natural stance and punch left hand choku zuki.*

24 *Bring left fist in front of and just below right shoulder, palm facing down . . .*

25   . . . bend right knee, lock left knee and twist hips to make a short zenkutsu dachi as you block left uche uke.

26   Step forward into kokutsu dachi. Twist hips and block shuto uke.

27   Step forward with left leg into kokutsu dachi and block shuto uke.

31   . . . use a strong elbow action to pull right hand down and across the body, whilst using left hand to augment this action. Hips should be rotated anti-clockwise at the same time.

32   Keeping hands in the same position and body square, raise right knee as high as possible . . .

33   . . . attack with a very low yoko geri kekomi (about knee height), simultaneously pulling both hands strongly to upper part of right side of chest. **KIAI** . . .

28 *Step forward with right leg into kokutsu dachi and block shuto uke.*

29 *Step back with right leg into kokutsu dachi and block shuto uke.*

30 *Straighten right leg and step across into zenkutsu dachi with left foot, taking both hands up and forward of left side of the head. The back of the right hand should face almost forward and the left fingertips should rest at the base of the right thumb . . .*

34 *. . . withdraw kicking leg back to knee-up position, turn head and cross hands in preparation for shuto uke . . .*

35 *. . . step back with right leg into kokutsu dachi and block chudan shuto uke.*

36 *Step forward with right leg into kokutsu dachi and block shuto uke.*

37 S-l-o-w-l-y withdraw right foot to left and pull right hand back to left hand, closing both fists.

38 Rear view of **37**.

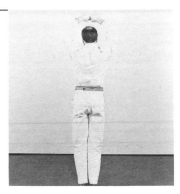

39 S-l-o-w-l-y lift both arms up, keeping fists together and rotating palms to the front. At the same time straighten the knees.

43 Thrust right leg forward and attack chudan zuki with right fist.

44 Rear view of **43**.

45 Look behind, move left leg across and take right hand up close to head with left hand down and behind. Both hands should be open . . .

40 *Pull both arms sharply outside to about shoulder-width, and at the same time quickly lift right knee.*

41 *Step forward with right leg and attack with morote tettsui uchi.*

42 *Rear view of **41**.*

46 *. . . twist into zenkutsu dachi, blocking jodan nagashi uke with left hand and attacking gedan nukite with right hand.*

47 *S-l-o-w-l-y shift weight to right leg; withdraw left leg to right leg with left foot parallel to right; straighten knees. Co-ordinate this with gedan barai with left hand, pulling right hand behind head to balance the left.*

48 *Turn body clockwise through 90° and raise right foot to jodan with right hand to left side of neck, left arm down across body . . .*

49   . . . stamp fumikomi and block gedan barai in kiba dachi.

50   Cross arms in front of chest with left hand open and left arm under, and look to left . . .

51   . . . s-l-o-w-l-y block with haishu uke.

55   Block gedan barai with right arm and support right elbow with left fist, palm facing up.

55a   Side view of **55**.

56   Block gedan barai with left arm and support left elbow with right fist, palm facing up.

52 *Rear view of* **51**.

53 *Twist hips through 90° and attack palm of left hand with right leg mika zuki geri . . .*

54 *. . . land in kiba dachi, rotating hips through a further 90° and attack palm of left hand with mawashi empi uchi.*

57 *Block gedan barai with right arm and support right elbow with left fist, palm facing up.*

58 *Step into zenkutsu dachi and pull hands back to left side, right hand on top.*

59 *Attack yama zuki (mountain punch) and lean body slightly forward to keep punches in line. Leaning action can also provide extra momentum for punches.*

135

59a   *Side view of* **59**.

60   *S-l-o-w-l-y withdraw right leg to feet-together position with hands to right side and upper body slightly pulled back.*

61   *Keeping body upright and arms in the same position, block with left leg mika zuki geri . . .*

64a   *Side view of* **64**.

65   *. . . step forward with right leg and as you land deliver yama zuki.*

66   *Step across with left leg and bring right arm high and left arm low. Look to front . . .*

62 . . . *step forward into zenkutsu dachi, and as you land deliver yama zuki.*

63 *S-l-o-w-l-y withdraw left leg to feet-together position with hands to left side and upper body slightly pulled back.*

64 *Again keeping body upright and arms held still, block jodan mika zuki geri with right leg . . .*

67 . . . *twist into zenkutsu dachi and swing right arm across groin, pulling left hand back to side.*

68 *Block gedan uche uke, using right forearm.*

69 *Step across with right leg, bring left arm up high and right arm down low . . .*

70 . . . *twist into zenkutsu dachi and swing left arm across groin, pulling right hand back to side.*

71 *Block gedan uche uke using left forearm.*

72 *Step with left leg half to two thirds to right leg and cross hands in preparation for shuto uke* . . .

76 . . . *step with left leg into kokutsu dachi and block shuto uke with* **KIAI.**

77 *Move left foot back to bring feet together. Bring hands together with left hand wrapped around right fist.*

78 *Step out with right foot to natural stance.*

73   . . . *step into kokutsu dachi with right leg and block shuto uke.*

74   *Keep kokutsu dachi and s-l-o-w-l-y pivot clockwise on left foot with right foot describing an arc until right foot is approximately shoulder-distance behind left foot. Whilst executing this movement, s-l-o-w-l-y rotate the head anti-clockwise. At the finish right foot and head should be facing exact opposite directions.*

75   *Move right foot to left foot with feet parallel and almost touching, and take hands to preparation position for shuto uke . . .*

Kumite (Sparring)

Introduction

Karate is essentially a martial art, and therefore all fundamental techniques need to be tested in a combat situation. Obviously it would be impractical to engage in serious combat, as karateka would hurt each other: consequently several formalized forms of sparring have evolved which may test relative skill with the minimum risk of injury. Whilst practising any type of kumite one must foster a martial attitude whilst showing respect for one's opponent's well-being.

Remember that this practice is for both of you, so you should work each other hard. For example, having announced a target, the attacker makes every attempt to reach that target. Your opponent has been told what attack to expect, and so their defence will be tested and improved by the speed and power of your attack. Undefended counter-attacks must be delivered with controlled vigour.

There are types of kumite which will test more specifically your understanding of distance and positioning for certain techniques, correct timing, and develop the way in which you react. Having developed all this, one can then hope to fight in a reasonably skilful manner. You should only embark on freestyle kumite when you have mastered the basic types of kumite.

One must always be respectful of one's opponent, and this is demonstrated right at the start of all kumite. This is the sequence which should start every type of kumite.

1 *Face each other in natural stance.*

2 *Bring feet together and place open hands at your side.*

3 *Bow deeply whilst maintaining eye contact.*

4 *Step back to natural stance.*

141

BOB POYNTON, 5TH DAN

Gohon Kumite
(Five-Step Sparring)

Introduction

Gohon kumite is a basic form of sparring which will teach and develop the fundamentals of body co-ordination in attacking and blocking. The exercise is formal and every stage must be executed following a predetermined routine. It is used in grading tests for the first three grades. Being so basic, it clearly tests understanding of co-ordination between step and hand techniques, stepping speed and balance. The routine is simple, allowing maximum concentration on quality.

GOHON KUMITE

Demonstrated by Bob Rhodes and Billy Higgins

1   *Both partners bow, keeping eye contact.*

2   *Both stand in natural stance, with the attacker having judged the correct distance.*

3   *The attacker steps back, with his right leg into zenkutsu dachi and simultaneously blocks gedan barai with the left arm. He now states clearly the target, which in this case is jodan (face).*

4   *Quickly and without warning, the first attack is made with jodan oi zuki, the defender reacting immediately by stepping back with his right leg into zenkutsu dachi and blocking age uke with his left arm.*

5   *The second attack is launched, this time with the left, which is again blocked, now with right-hand age uke.*

6   *The third attack, jodan oi zuki, is again blocked with age uke . . .*

143

7 . . . *as is the fourth attack* . . .

8 . . . *and the fifth attack.*

9 *The defender immediately delivers a counter-attack chudan gyaki zuki with* **KIAI**, *pulling the blocking arm strongly back to the opposite side.*

13 . . . *second attack and defence* . . .

14 . . . *third attack and defence* . . .

15 . . . *fourth attack and defence* . . .

10   *After pausing sufficiently to check distance and balance, the defender steps forward and the attacker back to natural stance. The roles are now reversed, with the same format as before repeated exactly . . .*

11   *The attacker steps back and states jodan . . .*

12   *. . . first attack and defence . . .*

16   *. . . fifth attack and defence . . .*

17   *. . . defender counter-attacks with* **KIAI** *. . .*

18   *. . . Again, after checking balance and distance, defender steps forward and attacker steps back to natural stance.*

145

19 . . . *Roles reverse once more; original attacker steps back with gedan barai and this time states the target as chudan (stomach).*

20 *As the attack is delivered, the defender steps back and this time blocks using chudan soto ude uke, taking care to block to the wrist and clear the attack from the body.*

21 *This is repeated with the left side . . .*

25 . . . *and followed immediately by chudan gyaku zuki to the stomach, delivered again with* **KIAI**.

26 *Again, after checking distance and balance, the defender steps forward and the attacker steps back to natural stance.*

27 *The roles are again reversed. The attacker steps back into zenkutsu dachi, blocks gedan barai and then states chudan.*

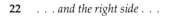

22   *. . . and the right side . . .*

23   *. . . again, with the left side . . .*

24   *. . . and the right side . . .*

28   *The five attacks are now returned to chudan and defended . . . first, with the right side . . .*

29   *. . . then left . . .*

30   *. . . then right . . .*

31   . . . then left . . .

32   . . . then right . . .

33   . . . and the final counter is delivered with **KIAI**.

34   Both opponents return to starting position, again with the defender stepping forward and the attacker stepping back.

35   The opponents bow to each other . . .

36   . . . and resume natural stance.

BOB POYNTON, 5TH DAN

Kihon Ippon Kumite (Basic One-Step Sparring)

Introduction

This is the type of kumite which develops both single attacks and blocks and counter-attacks. It is arguably the most practical form of sparring, as, for example, in competition sparring it is usually the single attack or counter-attack which will score the point. In a self-defence situation, it is quite often the first blow which will decide the outcome. If an attack is launched strongly and effectively, further defence becomes very difficult.

The attacker must state the technique and the target before attacking, and the defender may block and counter-attack with techniques of their own choice, or these may be decided by the instructor at that session. The main criteria when defending are as follows:

The block must be effective and the defender must remain on balance and be positioned correctly to deliver the counter-attack.

The counter-attack must be delivered immediately and not allow the attacker time to escape, defend or attack again.

The counter-attack must be delivered with full power and control to a carefully chosen target, mobilizing all possible parts of the body.

Each counter-attack must be delivered with *KIAI*.

KI HON IPPON KUMITE

Example A

1 *Bob Rhodes blocks Billy Higgins' attack by stepping back into zenkutsu dachi with age uke block, thus placing himself in a perfect position to counter-punch . . .*

2 *. . . which he does immediately, using a strong hip twist and retracting his opposite hand.*

Example B

1 *Frank Brennan steps inside Jimmy Brennan's chudan mae geri attack, blocking gedan barai . . .*

2 *. . . Exactly as Jimmy lands, Frank delivers a jodan gyaku zuki counter.*

150

Example C

1 *Terry O'Neill deflects Bob Poynton's chudan attack and immediately catches hold of his wrist . . .*

2 *. . . preventing Bob from escaping from his powerful jodan mae geri counter-attack.*

Example D

1 *Bob Poynton blocks Jimmy Poynton's chudan attack and makes an opening for his counter-attack . . .*

2 *. . . Bob simultaneously thrusts forward with yoko empi uchi whilst using his opposite hand to pull Jimmy more strongly on to the counter-attack.*

151

BOB POYNTON, 5TH DAN

Jiyu Ippon Kumite
(Semi-Freestyle One-Step Sparring)

Introduction

Jiyu ippon kumite is practised in a freestyle stance, and the attacker has the chance to move freely around their opponent. The advantage of such freedom is that the attacker may exploit any weakness in the opponent's concentration or balance, or if they don't exist, create them.

The defender in turn will try to exploit the commitment of the attacker to their own advantage.

The attacker still must state their target.

If the defender is able to time exactly when the attack will be delivered, they may simultaneously defend and counter-attack.

For the defender, this has two advantages: firstly, that during a committed attack it is difficult to think about blocking, and secondly, any counter-attack made against the attacker will be doubly effective because of the movement of the attacker's body onto the counter-attack.

This co-ordination of block and counter is not always possible, but if not simultaneously, the counter must be delivered immediately. Both attacker and defender must return to a kamae or ready position immediately.

Any block and counter-attack may be used, therefore, as long as they fulfil these criteria.

JIYU IPPON KUMITE

All the following examples begin from this position with both opponents carefully watching each other's movements. All counters are delivered with **KIAI**.

Example A

As Billy Higgins starts to attack with the right leg chudan mae geri, Andy Sherry thrusts in to simultaneously smother the kick and counter-punch chudan gyaku zuki.

Example B

1 *Frank Brennan blocks Jimmy Brennan's yoko geri kekomi attack, and in doing so spins Jimmy around . . .*

2 *. . . so that his back is presented as a clear target.*

Example C

As Bob Poynton attacks Terry O'Neill with chudan mae geri, Terry steps to the side and simultaneously delivers jodan mawashi geri to Bob's throat.

Example D

Bob Poynton leaps high to avoid Jimmy Poynton's chudan oi zuki attack, deflecting the punch down whilst at the same time striking to his neck with shuto uchi.

KAREN FINDLEY

Jiyu Kumite (Freestyle Kumite: Sports Kumite)

Karen Findley was European kumite champion in 1985 and 1986, and KUGB women's champion in 1986.

Preparation

I normally train about three times a week at my own club, Halewood, but if I have a competition coming up I do extra training. I start to prepare for an event about six weeks in advance. My training normally consists of set-piece sparring, practising a number of zuki and geri techniques using different footwork to disguise/speed up the techniques. We also do a lot of line-ups and mock competition fighting in groups of three, with each person taking their turn to referee. I concentrate on two to three of my favourite techniques and try to find different ways of making them work on different opponents.

At Halewood we have a very strong men's kumite team so I have a lot of experienced people to spar with. I am always at a disadvantage, because I have shorter arms and legs, but because of this I have to push myself harder to score. They all exercise good control when sparring with me, but they keep the sharpness in their attacks.

Kumite requires good distance, good timing and good footwork, but not neces-

sarily in that order – all are important as a package. You need to be able to attack from a long distance using good footwork to take you in fast, then fast out again to avoid injury.

When women's kumite was first introduced to competition at the Shotokan Cup in 1983, there were many injuries which seemed to occur because of poor fighting distance and footwork. On the word 'hajime', many of the contestants seemed to be drawn together like magnets, with fists and feet flying. Since then the standard has greatly increased, and the use of distance, timing and footwork are more apparent. I think that the women, including myself, now need to develop their 'fighting brain'. There are times when I have beaten opponents by strategy, but more often than not scoring has been a reaction rather than a planned move. I think that the introduction of women's team kumite matches would help to develop strategy.

The score and the position of the fighter dictates what action is needed. For example, if you are the fourth fighter and your team is winning 3–0, then you have no pressure to win because the result is already secured, and you can afford to settle down and use strategies to win the fight. If this doesn't work and you lose then it matters less. When you are fighting individually, you only have one chance and you can't afford to take any risks. Therefore you stick to your usual methods.

Coping with competition

The morning of a competition, I always start off with a good breakfast to see me through the day. You are often unsure of the time of your event, and as I don't like to compete on a full stomach I don't usually eat until after I've completed the eliminations.

I normally find that I'm particularly nervous during elimination rounds, but once I've worked my way through these I settle down and enjoy semi-finals and finals, and I usually fight much better. I find that my attitude plays a great part in how I perform. For example, if I haven't met the opponent before, but know that they are of a high

Karen Findley (left)

Kate Dyer

standard, then I fight much better. Sometimes if I'm facing people I have previously beaten, my attitude can become subconsciously casual and I'll make hard work of the fight.

Injuries

It is very difficult when you have an injury to know what is the best action to take – whether to train through it and risk making it worse, or whether to rest it completely and lose your fitness.

I am not a supple person and I have to push my body to its limits when training. Because of this I find I suffer from lots of strains and torn muscles. A torn back muscle put me out of training for a full two months. With this type of injury the only answer is to rest as the muscles in the back go into spasm and any slight movement causes great pain. I find osteopathy helps unlock muscles.

Competition in karate

I think it is important to practise karate as a whole with basics, kata and kumite as they all complement one another. I have watched other styles that have broken away to practise sports karate and nothing else. Their techniques appear to have become ineffective. There is a distinct lack of body power. Taking away the traditional part of the martial arts also appears to have taken away what I class as some of the most important parts, i.e. good attitude, respect and self-control.

Sports kumite is only a part of our martial art. Karate is for everyone from seven to seventy, and if sports kumite became the main aspect then we would find that karate only suited people in their teens and twenties.

However, an advantage is that by entering competitions you have a goal to aim for. When you are a kyu grade your goal is your grading every three months, but once you achieve dan grade there are long spells between each grading. Karate is not seasonal, like tennis or badminton. It is very difficult to work full-time and train week in week out year after year without going through bad patches when you have to push yourself hard to make your way to the dojo. I find that if I have an important competition coming up it is easier to shake off that feeling and knuckle down to training for the event.

GLOSSARY

age   rising (*age uke*, rising block)
ashi barai   leg sweep
bassai dai   kata first practised at brown belt level
budo   martial way
choku zuki   straight punch
chudan   chest (*choku zuki chudan*, straight punch to chest area)
dachi   stance (*zenkutsu dachi*, front stance)
dan   level of black belt
do   the way or path
dojo   the place of the way. Training area
empi   elbow (*empi uchi*, elbow strike)
fumikomi   stamping kick
gedan   lower body area (*gedan barai*, block to the lower body area)
gi   training suit
geri   kick (*mai geri*, front kick)
gyaku   reverse (*gyaku zuki*, reverse punch)
go   five (*go hon kumite*, five step sparring)
haito   ridgehand (*haito uchi*, ridgehand strike)
haishu   back of the hand (*haishu uke*, back of the hand block)
hajime   begin
heian kata   group of five basic katas (*heian shodan*, first basic kata in the heian group)
hidari   left side
jodan   head and neck area (*oi zuki jodan*, stepping punch to the head or neck)
jiyu ippon kumite   one-step semi-freestyle sparring
juji uke   x block
jiyu kumite   freestyle sparring
kamae   ready position
karate   empty hand fighting
karateka   practitioner of karate

kata   form or formal exercise
keage   snap kick (*yoko geri keage*, snap kick to the side)
kekomi   thrust (*yoko geri kekomi*, thrust kick to the side)
ki   power of the spirit
KIAI   a martial shout, to unite body and spirit
keri waza   kicking techniques
kiba dachi   side of straddle stance
kihon   basic (*kihon kumite*, basic sparring)
kizami zuki   jab punch
kokutsu dachi   back stance
kumite   sparring
kyu   level below black belt
ma-ai   distancing
mae   front (*mae geri*, front kick)
mawashi   roundhouse (*mawashi geri*, roundhouse kick)
mawate   turn
migi   right side
mika   crescent (*mika geri*, crescent kick)
mokusu   meditation
morote   two-handed (*morote uke*, two-handed block)
ni   two (*heian nidan*, second basic kata in the heian group)
nukite   spear hand
obi   belt
oi zuki   stepping or lunge punch
osae uke   pressing block
otoshi   downward (*otoshi empi uchi*, downward elbow strike)
rai   bow for courtesy and respect
seiza   kneeling or meditating position
sensei   teacher
shuto   knife hand (*shuto uke*, knife hand block)
sokumen uke   side two-handed block

soto uke block from the outside moving inward
tate upward (*tate shuto uke*, vertical upward knife hand block)
te hand
teisho palm heel (*teisho uke*, palm heel block)
tettsui bottom fist (*tettsui uchi*, bottom fist strike)
tsuki punching
uchi strike (*shuto uchi*, knife hand strike)
uche ude uke inside forearm block

ude forearm
uke block (*soto uke*, outside block)
uraken backfist
ushiro back, rear (*ushiro geri*, kick behind)
yama zuki u punch
yame stop
yoi be ready
yoko side (*yoko empi uchi*, side elbow strike, *yoko geri*, side kick)
zenkutsu dachi forward or front stance

The KUGB is a teaching organization which holds regular training courses for those who wish to improve their karate. Many are free to members, and they cover both basic and more advanced and specialized levels, including kata and kumite training and courses for refereeing and judging. There are three residential courses: Sensei Enoeda's course held at Crystal Palace National Sports Centre in May and September, the Lancaster karate summer school, and the Torbay spring kata course. For full details, please write to:

The Karate Union of Great Britain
Maychalk House
8 Musters Road
West Bridgford
Nottingham
Notts

For further reading, we recommend the bi-monthly *Fighting Arts International*, which carries full reports on all activities, and which should be available from any good newsagent. Subscription details can be obtained from:
Fighting Arts International
P O Box 26
Birkenhead
Merseyside L43 4Y Q

All equipment in this book has been kindly provided by Kamae Ltd. Those who wish to purchase equipment can write to:
Kamae International
Ewart Street
Saltney Ferry
Chester
Cheshire C H4 0B L   Tel: 0244 677534

Bob Poynton, 5th dan, is a senior instructor for the KUGB and serves on the National Technical and Executive Committees. He began training in 1965 at the world famous Liverpool Red Triangle Club, and now teaches there alongside KUGB chief instructor Andy Sherry. This dojo held the KUGB British title for seventeen years and has produced many outstanding karateka, including Terry O'Neill, Steve Cattle and Frank Brennan. Bob fought as a member of this team and represented the KUGB internationally for over seventeen years, winning many honours. In 1974 and 1982 he was named as the most outstanding European technician.

Caesar Andrews, 3rd dan, is a personal pupil of Sensei Enoeda. He is an instructor at Imperial, Eton and Wellington Colleges and for the Barbados National Karate Team, and he runs his own karate club. He has also taught members of the Metropolitan Police and the Grenadian Police Force.

Gary Day-Ellison is a brown belt and has been a student of Caesar Andrews since 1984. He has brought to this book a student's perspective to the challenges of karate and the most common problems faced.

Acknowledgements

Bob, Caesar and Gary wish to thank all those who helped in the production of this book, especially Sensei Enoeda and Sensei Sherry; the KUGB Technical and Executive Committees, in particular Charles Naylor and Derek Langham, Jimmy Brennan, Jimmy Poynton and Jim Murphy for providing their bodies as targets; Roy Victor and Carlo Faulds for their superb photographs; and Hilary Davies, Deborah Beale, Judith Hannam and Felicity Salmon at Pan Books for their help and patience.

First published 1988 by Pan Books Ltd, Cavaye Place, London SW10 9PG

9 8 7 6 5 4 3 2

© Caesar Andrews and Gary Day-Ellison 1988

ISBN 0 330 29783 X

Photoset by Rowland Phototypesetting Ltd, Bury St Edmunds, Suffolk

Printed and bound in Great Britain by Richard Clay Ltd, Bungay, Suffolk

Designed by Peter Ward

Photographs by Roy Victor © 1988
Photographs appearing on pages 78–139 by Carlo Faulds © 1988
Additional photographs by Carlo Faulds © 1988
Photographs on pages 2(c), 8, 11, 13 and 72 by Gary Day-Ellison © 1988
Photograph on page 156 by Kate Dyer © 1988